TULIPINA'S
Floral Fantasy

"Discovering the world of flowers was like embarking on a journey to art and its infinite possibilities, to the universe of colors, to the forms of architecture, to the heritage of history and literature . . . But, above all, it was an incredible journey to nature, the inexhaustible source of energy and wonder . . ."

TULIPINA'S Floral Fantasy

Magnificent Arrangements *and* Design Inspiration *from* World-Renowned Florist Kiana Underwood

ALESSANDRA MATTANZA *with contributions from* **KIANA UNDERWOOD**

PHOTOGRAPHS BY NATHAN UNDERWOOD

CHRONICLE BOOKS
SAN FRANCISCO

CONTENTS

FOREWORD
by Jose Villa

When flower art and design converge, it is a magical experience to see in person. Kiana Underwood has truly mastered her version of these floral creations. The depth and color choices are truly inspirational, taking you back to the golden age of Dutch paintings and a craft dating back to the sixteenth century, when flower choices were distinct in color and contrast. I like to refer to it as "where still life meets real life," as the breathtaking arrangements she creates bring this type of art full circle. Paintings of that era had a photorealistic effect, and for me as a photographer, capturing with my camera the flower arrangements that Kiana creates makes me feel like I am taking part in preserving history.

I met Kiana in 2016 and was immediately drawn to her kind spirit and amazing talent. Our friendship quickly evolved, and I started capturing her workshops in Italy, Austria, Mexico, and San Francisco, as well as having the pleasure of photographing several of her weddings. She creates elaborate works of art with flowers, and I have been mesmerized from day one. A truly beautiful human making such gorgeous floral designs—what's not to love? To just say I am proud of my friend for sharing her art is an understatement; I am profoundly and deeply grateful and honored to know her and witness her incredible craft. It is people like Kiana who bring inspiration to clients, to colleagues, to admirers, and to me, and I am honored to be a small part of this book, which will allow Kiana's magic and talent to continue to be shared with the rest of the world.

—Jose Villa,
celebrity wedding photographer

4–5 *In this composition, the colors flow in an irresistible contrast: cool green is balanced by a jaunty fuchsia, and the splashes of yellow and orange here and there further highlight the play of opposites.*
7 *Anything becomes more precious when "touched" by flowers, even the intense, dreamy gaze of a bride. Image courtesy of Jose Villa.*

A VOICE FOR FREEDOM AND ARTISTRY

by Kiana Underwood

> *"Woman is the light of God."*
>
> —*Jalaluddin Rumi*

There is one undeniable truth about the essence of who I am as a floral artist, and that is where I come from. The culture, rich history, poetry, and music I have been gifted as an Iranian woman are at the heart of my flower creations.

My childhood experiences, as well as a love for Persian literature and music, have been the driving force for all that I do in life. I dedicate this book to the amazing and brave women of my motherland of Iran, who have been fighting tirelessly to break the shackles of more than forty years of oppression and tyranny by the Islamic Republic. May the light of the great poet Omar Khayyam be with you, and may you prevail.

Zan. Zendegi. Azadi.

—*Kiana*

9 *An homage to the Iranian people—a show of solidarity in Milan for the freedom of Kiana's motherland—for women, life, freedom, and a free Iran, inspired by the beautiful image of Forough Alaei (@foroughalaei) taken for Time. Image courtesy of Umberto Armiraglia.*

SHE IS MY ROCK STAR

by Nathan Underwood

For me, she is just Kiana: my wife, mother of my children, and best friend. For twenty-five years, we have been partners in this adventure called life, and for the past twelve years, in this evolution of floral beauty known as Tulipina.

If you had asked me when I first met Kiana—in an Italian class at the University of California, Santa Barbara—whether I thought she would someday be one of the most sought-after and artful floral designers on the planet, I might have laughed. However, if you had asked me, "Is Kiana a bold, tenacious, driven woman?" that would have been easy—the answer to that question has always been a resounding *yes*. So it should have come as no surprise when—once our children were no longer very young—she took her talent for making beautiful arrangements around the house and started Tulipina. In very little time, Kiana had people from all over the world interested in what she was doing.

Some people are born to paint, draw, sing, or play a sport—it is their calling, and this purpose and passion fuels and drives their spirit. This is true of Kiana. She was born to paint with flowers and amazes me regularly with her ability to evolve, innovate, and push the boundaries of what it means to be an artist.

She is my rock star and, undoubtedly, the queen of floral design.

—Nathan

INTRODUCTION
THE ENCHANTMENT OF FLOWERS
by Alessandra Mattanza

For some, life is an adventurous journey of self-discovery. These people keep their minds open to new possibilities and opportunities. Rather than being afraid of change, they trust in it, with their heart full of hope and heads full of dreams. They let their instincts and passions guide their lives, just as a leaf floats in the wind. On the journey to discover new perspectives, new places, and new experiences, experimentation offers fertile ground for personal and creative growth.

Kiana Underwood is one of these extraordinary souls. Her path to discovering herself as an artist took lots of twists and turns, but once she discovered her identity as a floral artist, she found her true happiness. This discovery made her life shine with light, colors, and new ideas. Her winding journey to get here, full of varied experiences around the world, allowed Kiana to realize the passion that sets her soul on fire. It is clear from the look in her eyes and from her words as she tells her story, which sounds like a fairy tale. And of course, fairy tales have their share of obstacles and dark times before the happy ending.

Like all visionaries, Kiana is driven by a thirst for knowledge; like all explorers, she is bewitched by new, eye-opening cultural experiences; like all Romanticists, she is consumed by memories from the past; like all artists, she is fascinated by the miracles and opportunities of the present. In many ways she is a sort of contemporary Alice in Wonderland, venturing into a realm of her own, made of shapes, materials, and diverse means of expression, revealing her wonderful inner world. Her creations are a combination of reinvented and rediscovered beauties, sometimes even a meeting point of art and technique, which unfolds and unwinds in an image, like the buds of cherry trees that suddenly blossom in spring, making every tree a triumph of beauty and joy. Her creations give expression to unspoken memories, accomplishing an extraordinary transformation.

The details in her floral masterpieces stand out, as powerful as a painting by Caravaggio, and the design evolves into a perfect asymmetry of seductive, almost geometric forms reminiscent of an abstract masterpiece by Picasso. Kiana is skillful at evoking emotions, fantasies, and suggestions, in a succession of joy and happiness and an incredible exaltation of the senses reminiscent of some paintings by Botticelli, or the rising and falling piano notes of a Bach composition. As in a magic kaleidoscope, her works offer an unconventional explosion of colors. As you take in her creations from different angles, the perspective changes with each new view. Contemplating a rose or noticing the detail of a ranunculus, you lose yourself more and more among the shapes and combinations of the elements, which, depending on the mood and season, might include apples, berries, tomatoes, strawberries, blackberries, raspberries, herbs, and whatever else nature can offer to play, improvise, create, and recreate with. Kiana likes to constantly change, experiment, innovate, and evolve, embracing new forms of expression.

My first encounter with Kiana's floral magic came when I saw a display of roses, my favorite flower. I was immediately drawn to her rose creations because they aroused a wide range of emotions in me. The Indian philosopher Inayat Khan believed that roses could be compared to the human soul: "The soul becomes like a rose and begins to show the rose quality. Just as the rose consists of many petals held together, so the person who attains to the unfoldment of the soul begins to show many different qualities. These qualities emit fragrance in the form of a spiritual personality. The atmosphere of the spiritual being pervades the air like the perfume of the rose. The rose has seeds in its heart, and so the developed souls have in their heart that seed of development which produces many roses."

I find scarlet red roses particularly bewitching and fascinating, with their extraordinary power to evoke secret romances and great loves. A beautiful Arabic legend tells that a long, long time ago all roses were white, until one night a nightingale casually came to rest in a rose garden, and he fell so madly in love with these flowers that he started singing for them. Inebriated by their scent, he pressed his chest so hard against a rose that he was pierced by one of its thorns. Unable to contain his passion, he continued to sing and sing, until he ended up making the rose brightly red with his blood.

In every country and for each flower there are beautiful, moving, and often heartbreaking stories, myths, and fairy tales, and I am sure that the emotions and drama captured in these legends can be found in Kiana Underwood's creations. While looking at Kiana's floral arrangements, you might first just take in the aesthetic side—the external beauty, the balance, the range of lovely ingredients—but if you look deeper, you will notice that the arrangements are speaking to you, evoking emotions, memories, and inspiration. And if you stop to admire them a little bit longer, you may be surprised to discover that each arrangement tells a story.

This is Kiana's unique art, and it is this characteristic that distinguishes her style from all the others. Her creations can speak to the soul of the viewer just as eloquently as a painting or sculpture. It is as if each flower, each element of the arrangement, has its own role in a magnificent theatrical piece, leading its audience to reflect, compare the past and the present, and think about what is yet to come. Her floral creations are like a book to leaf through, page after page, in search of a plot that goes beyond words.

Kiana has a gift for creating moments of enchantment and pure poetry. The wealth of details, the asymmetric whole, the vulnerability, and the ephemeral nature of the creation itself turn her arrangements into true art, her iconic events into unique moments that can be immortalized only in a photograph, captured in an indelible image. And so, Kiana's ideas, which she turns into the most eclectic inventions, are inspired by the magic of being able to capture the fleeting moments, as well as by the precariousness and vulnerability of existence. It is then that the eye gets lost in a maze of colors and feelings, and Kiana remembers to seize and live in the moment in her free creative fever and boundless enthusiasm.

Her winding journey to becoming a world-renowned floral artist evokes a passage from Steve Jobs's 2005 commencement speech at Stanford University: "You can't connect the dots looking forward; you can only connect them looking backward. So, you have to trust that the dots will somehow connect in your future. You have to trust in something—your gut, destiny, life, karma, whatever. This approach has never disappointed me, and it made the difference in my life."

In these pages, we'll look back on the dots that led Kiana to become one of the most beloved and celebrated floral artists of our time. Through engaging storytelling, expert wisdom, and hundreds of gorgeous images, you'll discover how memory, art, place, music, and more have contributed to her signature style. And as you see her journey unfold, the hope is that you will be inspired to draw on your memories, experiences, and passions to create your own distinct floral fantasies and elevate life's moments with botanical beauty.

A LIFETIME OF INSPIRATION

An Artist's Journey Through
Cultures, Colors, and Fragrances

THE PAST AND MEMORY, THE CHARM OF REMEMBRANCE

"I think of my flower arrangements as 'painting with flowers.' When I begin, the canvas is blank, and the flowers and foliage are my one-of-a-kind paintbrushes."

"My relationship with the universe of flowers is now an integral part of my soul," Kiana says. "But, just as in one of the many Persian fairy tales I used to listen to as a child, it gets lost in time, among different experiences, journeys, and adventures.

"It begins with my memories, with the earliest childhood emotions; it has its roots in the traditions of my country, and of the culture I come from, which will always be part of me, wherever I go." But despite this deep, profound connection to flowers, they didn't become a central part of her life until she was thirty. "I certainly would never have imagined that they would play such an important role in my destiny, even though I was already bewitched and maybe influenced by them."

Persian Roots

Kiana's journey has taken her from Iran to San Francisco, from Italy to Paris, and beyond, each place offering her experiences that find their way into her work. Today, she splits her time between the magical woods and mountains of New York's Hudson Valley, where she carefully tends her own personal garden of floral wonders, and Lake Como, in Italy, which she considers her adopted country and source of romantic inspiration. She considers the United States her home, and also the place of her regeneration, where she discovered her full potential and evolved as a woman and an artist—the place where everything really began for her.

But Kiana's deepest roots will always be in her Persia, engraved in her mind and heart, painful but inspiring.

For her, Persia was a place of magical, almost enchanted, landscapes and villages, but also of tragedies and suffering. Both the magic and the turmoil of her time in Persia are visible in her art through the bright colors, the sometimes melancholic shadowy displays, and the unpredictable explosions of flowers, leaves, branches, and fruits. These elements contribute to the unique style that is now celebrated by her many fans all over the world.

Her earliest memories are of a brief period of happiness enjoyed with her loved ones—a happiness that was abruptly interrupted by the violent conflicts and political and social dramas that have marked the recent history of Iran. The light and shadows of these experiences will always exert a strong influence on her life path and choices.

"I consider myself Persian, because you can never forget your homeland, and my Persia was a wonderful country. Tehran was full of beautiful gardens, just as you read in many fairy tales or see in movies. Since ancient times, flowers, fragrances, and colors have always been an important part of the Persian culture. I still have vivid memories of this, memories that forcefully come to my mind while I am creating a floral arrangement, just as they often visit me at night, in my dreams."

Kiana remembers her grandfather's wonderful garden, adorned with pots of lush geraniums, and several greenhouses where he used to shelter a wide variety of plants and flowers. "When I close my eyes and think of him, I can still smell in my nostrils the scent of the earth, the leaves, and the petals. Those were my first steps in the floral universe," she remembers, with a sigh of nostalgia. Her grandmother would place delicate dried flowers between the pages of her books, as if they were precious jewels. Opened later, the book could unexpectedly still emanate an amazing scent. "Most certainly, it is from her that I learned to appreciate scents."

Scents are central to so many of Kiana's childhood memories. "I still remember today, with the same intensity, the scent of the jasmine that used to reign supreme in Iran on summer afternoons. We used to spend our holidays on the Caspian Sea, where my parents had a little house. I was eight, and I liked immersing myself in the nature that grew lush in the garden and all around our house, which was full of wildflowers whose bright colors used to catch my eye and tremendously fascinate me. All these experiences will always be part of me. I used to take them for granted back then, but over time, and during my growing-up process—which includes essential stages of life like having become a wife and then a mother, having created a solid family, and having found my career path—they have become more and more precious. The past and the present have mingled in a wonderful constellation that spurs me to explore with confidence the new opportunities that the future may hold."

Kiana's early childhood experiences represent two antithetical worlds. "From the first one I remember the happiness and serenity of everyday family life, and the confidence inspired by cultural traditions, in which we were deeply immersed; from the second one I remember the fear and horror." In 1979, when Kiana was only four years old, revolution broke out in Iran. "I perfectly remember, as if it were still echoing in my ears, the terrible racket that ripped the air and the sudden screams of people, and I remember the fear for my destiny and that of my family that used to squeeze my heart. Then, the advent of the dictatorship marked the end of our society—and the end of my enchanted universe and naivety."

Children who witness war often have to grow up faster than their peers. This was true of Kiana. "In 1981, the war between Iran and Iraq broke out. From that moment, everything in my life and my childhood changed." Her family had to flee Tehran to seek refuge in the countryside. "I still remember the sound of sirens at night and the people crowding the streets, desperately trying to flee," she says. It was then that she learned to listen to the wisdom of the elderly. "My father kept telling me: 'Never close the window!' But I was scared of what was happening outside, and so one night I closed the window and that very night we were bombed. It was only then that I realized why I shouldn't have closed the window. The shattered windowpanes were scattered all over the room. I, by some miracle, was not wounded. But that noise will always stick with me, deeply rooted in my memory. In that precise moment I understood the ineluctable power of destiny and the measureless immensity of human fragility."

Surrounded by devastation and despair, Kiana's parents decided to leave Iran. "We arrived in England, but my father was unable to get a job, and we were forced to return to our homeland," she recalls with great sadness.

Back in Iran, it was not easy for Kiana to find her way in a society crushed by the weight of dictatorship and characterized by extremely discriminatory attitudes toward women. Even at home, life was not easy, as she explains: "My father was very strict and, like my sister, I have always had a conflicted relationship with him. But what mostly weighed on me was having to attend school under a regime of Islamic fanatics. It was a horrible experience. I felt like I was in prison; I felt suffocated and misunderstood. I hated school. It was then that I understood the importance of freedom."

Kiana learned to face the vicissitudes of life by surrounding herself with the people and things she loved, knowing how to see the bright side in every situation, having patience, and learning the art of waiting, ready to bloom as soon as the opportunity presented itself.

She began to seek refuge in poetry, literature, and the art of calligraphy. "It was art that saved me, giving me a reason to go on living and offering me a glimmer of hope amid so much darkness. I used to retreat into that 'enchanted garden' and isolate myself from everything around me."

She found herself drawn to the words of the eleventh-century poet Omar Khayyam: "I considered him a sort of courageous revolutionary, and I loved his sensitivity toward love and the precariousness of life, his bold honesty in grasping reality and dealing with death, and his natural instinct for capturing the fleeting moments. I used to take some comfort also from traditional Iranian music, which for me was like a partial antidote to sadness. The Islamic government had banned pop music, and so I rediscovered traditional melodies and fell in love with them. I loved classical music with the same intensity, Beethoven and Bach in particular, and I also started playing the piano and writing poetry, paying particular attention to calligraphy, which to me was a sort of meditative practice."

Flowers, too, offered moments of pleasure. Kiana's bedroom had a window facing the garden, which served as almost a portal. "In summer, I used to open the window, and the scents that reached me evoked magical emotions and images of distant worlds. Around five in the evening, when the sun was beginning to set and the hour of twilight approached, the scents used to abruptly change in the dreamy interlude when the day meets the night." She began to collect the flower seeds and plant them in the family's garden, just beneath her window so she could smell them from her room.

The garden offered her respite from the challenges of everyday life. "I kept having trouble at school. I felt so alone, I was sad and depressed, and that garden helped me keep my mind off things." Her mother, too, found joy and relief in the garden. "My mother was a wonderful soul, full of optimism and love of life. She, too, had her own little garden, where she used to seek refuge from the daily problems and worries. She loved hyacinths and tuberoses, flowers full of enchanting fragrances." But while Kiana had a vision for a better world and better circumstances for women, she did not sense that her mother questioned their circumstances in Iran. "Unlike me, she used to just accept things, without wondering why—after all, back then that situation was common among all women. However, I was already unconsciously fighting for myself and my independence."

Blooming in California

When she was fifteen, Kiana and her family left Iran for San Francisco. She recalls, "This for me represented a fundamental change from a personal point of view, that would also influence my future professional choices. It was a very bright moment, a moment of rediscovery of myself, of productivity and the will to live and find my identity. Before that moment, my story had been an intense, hard-fought, difficult, and tragic one."

It was in San Francisco that Kiana experienced her first great rebirth. She found herself catapulted from fundamentalist Iran into the heart of the hippie culture. "In San Francisco, I learned to rediscover myself, to become self-confident, and I bloomed as I never imagined I would."

For the first time she could remember, Kiana found herself enjoying school, receiving kindness and support from her teachers. "My teachers became my best friends, inspiring and helping me as I grew up. I also found a sense of community." She joined the school choir and found an inspiring teacher who helped her cultivate her artistic passion and talent. For a young girl fleeing from a dark, oppressive place, the San Francisco community offered the chance to explore her potential, better understand others, develop a profound empathy, and be respected and appreciated.

Kiana was inspired and motivated by her precocious classmates, many of whom were also immigrants. "My class was multiethnic, with a strong presence of girls who were very ambitious and encouraged me to constantly improve myself." She didn't speak English very well yet, but she wasn't the only one, and the young newcomers supported each other. It really was a new world, a new frontier for them, where they could move forward, together and strong, in a free and democratic society that offered endless opportunities.

"In San Francisco, the past and the present mingled in an incredible harmony, as in a perfect musical melody,"

Kiana recalls. "There was a strong adventurous and exploring spirit in the air, and a wonderful world opened up before my eyes, with amazing gardens sometimes hidden behind gates or in unexpected yards, and huge parks full of trees and flowers, like a universe full of opportunities and based on equality and freedom."

Back then, she never imagined that flowers would be part of her professional future, but they certainly were all around her. Though her family no longer had their own garden, they found other ways to embrace nature's beauty in their new city. "Every day my mother used to buy fresh flowers to decorate the house with. As soon as my father got a job, we moved to a house in the Stonestown neighborhood, not far from the ocean and the wonderful Ocean Beach, which I soon discovered was surrounded by endless flowers and wild nature.

"San Francisco will always be dear to me because it brought me back to life." She acknowledges San Francisco's well-known cold summers and persistent fog, but also how the gray was enlivened by the bright colors of the flowers at the markets, the flowerbeds, the towering eucalyptus trees, and the botanical garden in Golden Gate Park. She discovered Sausalito, a waterfront town with a strong Mediterranean spirit reminiscent of Italy or France and graced with gardens, as well as Mt. Tamalpais and its ridges, valleys, and mature forests, including the coastal redwoods in Muir Woods, with their towering, massive trunks.

After high school, Kiana enrolled at the University of California at Santa Barbara. "Being far from home, living alone, and discovering my independence was the best thing that could have happened to me: I learned who I really was and discovered my full potential. Back then, I aspired to become a lawyer and fight for human rights. I wanted to make a real difference, to defend the weak, especially women, against oppression and discrimination. I wanted to travel and explore the world, to live and work in other countries."

"Anyone can create an installation or arrangement stuffed with flowers, but abundance with specific intention appears effortless and artful without being ostentatious."

Romance in Italy

She had always fantasized about spending time in Italy, so when she learned of a study abroad exchange program in Siena, she jumped at the opportunity. Kiana's arrival in Italy marked the beginning of a second rebirth.

"The time I spent in Siena was one of the best periods of my whole life. The study program lasted only two and a half months, but I learned a lot, and it was very stimulating from an artistic and creative point of view. I became so fond of this country's culture that I started studying Italian. Italy reminded me in many ways of the wonderful Persia of my childhood, and for me it still represents a powerful love story."

She loved taking excursions outside the city walls. "Whenever I ventured out in the countryside, I discovered wonderful golden wheat fields where thousands of poppies created an amazing design. I liked being photographed under the arbors of blooming wisteria—I can almost still smell their fragrance."

Kiana had fallen deeply in love with Italy, but she did not yet know that her passion for the Italian language would lead her to meet the love of her life. Back in Santa Barbara after the exchange program, she began studying Italian, and during a course called "How to find a job in Italy" she met her husband-to-be, Nathan Underwood. "We were taught how to talk on the phone and interact with people. We used to have fun and joke," Kiana remembers. "There was a creative and infectious cheerfulness in the air, but Nathan was always very serious."

Nathan describes himself as an introvert who has always had a penchant for technology. "Back then, I was working toward a degree in music, and I used to play drums. I had to choose a language to be able to continue my specialization path, and Italian had a good rhythm."

Smiling, Kiana recalls that "Nathan was the nerdiest in the class, but he was extremely kind and empathetic. There was a deep and disarming strength in him that inspired tenderness. He was only twenty-two, but he was already incredibly independent and reliable: You could feel that you could count on him. We developed a good friendship, and after I returned to San Francisco, we started writing long letters and emails, sharing our daily experiences."

Kiana and Nathan seem to relate to each other like the notes of a perfect musical harmony both personally and professionally. Though their personalities are quite different, their complementary strengths and common values and interests brought them together. They shared a passion for Italy and music, and also a strong social commitment. "I've always been shy," says Nathan, "so it has always been difficult for me to openly show my feelings. But in the end, what we felt for each other clearly emerged, and in 1998 our relationship officially began."

Soon after that, Kiana found her way back to Italy, through a prestigious program at Johns Hopkins University's campus in Bologna.

"Inspiration comes from emotions, memories, journeys, places, and impressions of the moment."

"I loved the fact that Bologna wasn't constantly overrun by tourists, and that you could feel like you were in the most appealing and authentic heart of Italy. I also loved that predominant earthy red color, and the architecture characterized by colonnades and beautifully harmonizing and contrasting elements and details. I was also fascinated by the scents that filled the air, especially those of food, evoking suggestions and promises of flavors and temptations." Bologna profoundly influenced the artistic sensibility that was steadily unfolding within her.

She also drew inspiration from nearby Florence. Taking in its architectural beauty, she was truly bewitched by the power of art, perhaps for the first time, and she fully understood its beauty. "For me Florence was a continuous discovery of perfect beauty, balanced shapes, wonderful suggestions, and great personal inspiration," Kiana says. "My mother taught me to appreciate the scent of flowers, and the air in Florence was filled with their fragrance. It was as if their petals were wheeling and dancing, full of promises in the wind, just like in those Botticelli paintings that I deeply love."

In 2000, Kiana and Nathan got engaged on the highest floor of the Eiffel Tower in Paris, a city that has always been a source of inspiration for them both. "I deeply loved the flower markets and beautiful cafes. Paris bewitched me with its powerful creative vein and its colors, like the red of geraniums that reigned supreme on the balconies."

A Creative Rebirth

Upon returning to the United States, Nathan and Kiana got married, and Kiana started a job at the Hoover Institution's research center at Stanford University. But she knew something was missing.

And then came motherhood. "Maternity gave me joy, happiness, and optimism, and filled me with a new burst of energy. It was another great period of rebirth. I had three children within five years. Our home and our daily lives changed: A new phase had begun," Kiana says. Motherhood gave her a chance to take a step back and reflect on what she wanted to do next.

During this phase, flowers began to play a more central role in her life. "While I was at home looking after my children, I used to have fun creating floral arrangements and taking care of my garden, just as my grandparents used to do when I was a child."

As she designed arrangements for her home, she found herself falling deeply in love with this art form. "I was passionate about the flowers' shapes, their colors, and their essence. When I first started using them to adorn my home in San Francisco, or to brighten up the table and some corners that seemed a little bit dull, everything shone with new life. It was then that I fully understood the true power of flowers and found my way."

Parents of her children's friends saw her work and began to ask her to make arrangements and installations for them, and Kiana realized she had a special talent for floral design. She decided to take the leap and start her own company.

"I loved being a mother, but I also needed something that could be entirely mine. I wanted something that could make me happy and define me. That's when I came up with the idea of becoming a floral designer, and Nathan encouraged me, telling me that I wouldn't lose anything by trying. Of course, being surrounded by love made me feel self-confident and gave me courage. I wasn't young enough to start a new profession from scratch, and I knew it, but I felt I could do something important. I wanted to explore, to find an outlet for my imagination again, to travel to a new universe: a garden of wonders made of colors, fragrances, and feelings. I put my heart and soul into reinventing myself with my business, and I loved every moment of this new adventure. I found out who I really was, and I knew the best was yet to come."

"A tulip may easily have three or four different nuances, and each is unique in the point of its petals, its stem, and its overall look. In general, when I start working, I take the flowers and look at them closely to discover their singularities, their unique characteristics. It is by focusing on this that my creations often start to come to life. Most of the time, the more varied it is, the more beautiful it will be. I like tulips, but I adore ranunculus, as I think they best represent my personality for their variations of color and shape, and for their resilience."

FLORAL
DESTINY

A Style Defined by Memories,
Ingredients, and Color

THE MOMENT AND DISCOVERY,
THE SONG OF COLOR

*"*When designing, one of the best ways to create unique inspiration is to look closely at the flowers. Close attention to the color combinations and delicate nuances reveals that each individual flower—much like each completed arrangement—is like no other.*"*

Discovering our individual tastes and preferences is a journey of self-discovery. How do we decide that one thing in our life is more important than another? How do we let something, or someone, seduce us? Sometimes it is love at first sight; other times it is a love that needs time to blossom, and when it does, it becomes powerful, obsessive, undeniable, like a fire that warms the soul as if it were the source of life.

"I didn't understand it for far too long, but now I know that flowers are everything to me." Realizing that her destiny was in flowers, Kiana officially turned her passion into a floral design business in 2011. The name, Tulipina, was inspired by her love of Italy. "I wanted to come up with an original and Italian name, because Italy had always been in my destiny. Tulipina called to my mind a tiny female floral creature. Even if I find tulips interesting, I wouldn't include them in the list of my favorite flowers, so the choice was neither influenced nor determined by tulips in any way. Rather, I loved the sound that this name produced in uttering it; it sounded like the title of a song or a poem."

"Discovering the floral world has been like embarking on a journey into art and its endless possibilities, into the universe of colors, the shapes of architecture, and the heritage of history and literature. But above all, it has been an incredible journey into nature, an inexhaustible source of energy and wonder."

*"*I consider every season an opportunity to create something new and original. Every season can give me new ideas, inspiring me and constantly pushing me to evolve my art.*"*

Memories and Symbols

As she developed Tulipina's aesthetic, Kiana found herself inspired by memories and experiences from her childhood. Flowers have always represented a fundamental aspect of Iran's culture, and each has a precise meaning and a particular function. For example, rose water, made from roses, is still sprayed on guests as a sign of good wishes. Roses are also considered a symbol of boundless love and affection. The lotus flower is considered a symbol of spiritual growth. According to ancient legends, Anahita, the Persian deity of water, health, and fertility, was born from a lotus flower.

In Persian literature, the narcissus, because of its shape and bright color, is often associated with the pupils of a beloved person. Pansies evoke sad feelings and romantic inspiration. As in cultures all over the world, flowers are commonly used to celebrate important life events, such as engagements, weddings, birthdays, and, the beginning of a new year (in Iran, Nowruz). Even though Kiana has not been to Iran for a long time, all these cultural memories are vivid in her mind. "I still remember the floral decorations for the first day of the year or the first day of spring. They both were really important moments in our culture. I loved each spring—the great rebirth after the winter slumber."

"A flower arrangement with an eclectic combination of colors like pink, orange, yellow, green, violet, and pure white can be reminiscent of a dream. Life is just a dream, and so what's better than making it as beautiful as possible? In the end, we all are the memories we leave behind us."

These memories have contributed to creating her unique style, characterized by one-of-a-kind, unpredictable, and inimitable arrangements that spontaneously spring from her, a combination of passion, instinct, and attention to detail. According to her, flowers have different personalities, just like human beings, and as such must be respected, because it is often the simplest and perhaps the humblest flower that reveals the greatest charm.

Kiana has always loved showcasing a diverse range of ingredients, and she finds variety interesting, often working with unusual flowers, which she sometimes juxtaposes with other natural elements, such as branches, fruits, vegetables, and leaves. For her, Mother Nature is a precious treasure from which to draw freely.

Hearing her talk about flowers, you can sense the thoughtfulness she brings to each ingredient—its personality and its place in an arrangement. "Ranunculus are probably the flowers I love the most, which is why they are often present in my floral arrangements. They come in many different colors; they are versatile and adaptable in different contexts. I also love their ability to live and bloom for a long time: they often become more and more beautiful as they open after the first cut. It is not easy to find this quality in flowers."

Kiana notes that there are enough different floral species to meet anyone's demands. She is fascinated by poppies, for one. "I've always thought they are the flowers of happiness. They are elegant but cheerful, and they endow arrangements with movement, adding a unique and charming design touch. Bellflowers can be extremely beautiful as well, and so perfect that they look fake. Jasmines have an extraordinary scent that can conquer the senses and infuse one with an incredible feeling of well-being."

Often her arrangements reflect nature's rhythms and moods. "I like all seasons of the year and all their manifestations in their natural sequence, which also marks the rhythm of our lives. Winter is a time for reflection, but also experimentation, often through exoticism, because I often feel the need to use flowers that blossom in distant corners of the world where cold does not exist. Spring is the time of promises, love, and rebirth. Summer is the adventure of nature's triumph, the time of parties, holidays, fun, and letting ourselves go. Fall is perhaps my favorite season, with its leaves tinged with a thousand colors and myriad fruits full of promises, which I use in a way very similar to flowers."

48-49 *Lots of different armchairs and lots of bright-colored flowers create a truly timeless location. Image courtesy of Corbin Gurkin.*
49 *Other natural elements, such as pumpkins, sometimes accompany the flowers to set the stage.*

"In my creations I always like to use flowers of different shapes and textures. I believe this lends the arrangement an interesting element that captures an observer's attention, inspiring them to reflect."

"When I know that an arrangement has to last only a day or so, I like to improvise. In these cases, there is nothing I love working with more than fully open flowers. There is no better tool for design than a flower at the very peak of its beauty. The joy of the fleeting moment lends it a singular elegance. The precariousness of existence melds with the duration of the day. In my arrangements, I often enjoy adding fruit, an element seen in certain still lifes that live forever on the canvas—just as I hope that my work may endure in a picture or a book."

"I chose international relations as the focus area for my graduate studies, because I dreamed of traveling and discovering the world. Many years and three children later, I travel the world to bring everywhere my creations. I am so grateful for this opportunity and couldn't ask for a better way to follow my dreams. I believe the greatest luck in life is to be able to love what you do, and the icing on the cake is the places you can work and the people you have the pleasure of collaborating with."

51 *What is poetry? It may be petals opening shyly or stems bending slightly, as if bowing, or maybe a few bunches of grapes to cheer everything up.*
52 *Sometimes a bouquet of flowers can explode with energy and vitality, giving whoever sees it a burst of joyful emotion.*
54 *In this arrangement, the flowers all seem to be talking to each other, facing each other so they can chat among themselves.*
55 *How many shades of a color can you find in a flower? Orange, for example, can be enriched with peach or salmon or coral tones, but also with yellow, sand, and many others.*

Color

In Kiana's floral universe, color is often a guiding force behind her designs. "There are countless shades of colors," she observes, "and while it's true that some colors can more easily be found in certain seasons, with a bit of creativity you can always create something special and unique throughout the year—you just have to rely on your imagination." Her ebullient spirit leads her to experiment and have fun with every flower she chances upon, giving them personality, almost humanizing them. "I let the goal of the whole arrangement guide me, not relying on any particular color alone."

Kiana doesn't restrict herself to just primary colors, but broadens her horizons by using all the variations and nuances that nature offers, always discovering new ones and giving life to an endless range of colors that she uses to give shape to her art. When considering color, she thinks about tone, dimension, and meaning:

Black: It is not easy to find a wide variety of black flowers in nature, but that's exactly why the arrangements created with them can be so surprising and wonderful for Kiana. "In summer, I prefer chocolate brown dahlias, *Angelica sylvestris* 'Purpurea', black tomatoes, or crepe myrtle. In early spring, the new foliage of plums may be helpful, as may some quite rare black primroses with a yellow center, and we must not forget the tulips. Fall is the best season for a dark-toned floral palette, with grapes whose purple is so intense that it becomes almost black, or dark pansies, orchids, potato vine, and coleus leaves. In winter, there are the checkered lilies (*Fritillaria*), with their bellflowers that seem to dance elegantly and charmingly in the air."

White: Kiana associates this color with romance and tradition. "For me, it's strongly linked to the feminine world. I often use white vases. I love lilies, poppies, anemones, roses, ranunculus, and the white leaves of ivy. In summer, there are the beautiful magnolias and the gardenias. In fall, I am bewitched by Japanese anemones and begonias. In winter, I have enjoyed creating arrangements with the bell tree dahlia (*Dahlia imperialis*), the narcissus, with its intense scent, and the peony."

Pink: Pink symbolizes romantic love, sweetness, and femininity. "It is very easy to find pink in nature, in a range of many different nuances that enable me to play with this color as I please. I've always enjoyed waiting for the different stages of flowering. Sometimes I like using the dogwood, which I make stand out to evoke asymmetry. Also tulips, with their long stems that can be allowed to arc, are perfect for this purpose—and they have a strong personality. In summer, I love to play with the different shapes of begonias. In fall, I let myself be inspired by dahlias, with their many different shapes and dimensions that create marvelous variations. In winter, I'm devoted to orchids, whose color in this season is full of delicacy and tenderness."

Peach: Peach tones often appear in Kiana's arrangements. If their color is more pastel, they evoke sweetness and friendship; if they are more intense, they symbolize energy and vitality. Peach tones might be just a shade of pink for some, but not for Kiana. "For me, spring is the season of this color, when I usually have fun matching tulips, narcissus, pansies, and poppies. In summer, there are many peach-colored dahlias, and sometimes I add eucalyptus leaves, carnations, viburnums, and, again, poppies. Sometimes I even use peaches, which I love to combine with roses that I pick in my garden by the end of summer. In winter, I find poinsettias really evocative, and the peach-colored ones are absolutely amazing."

58 Each color has its own meaning, which can vary from person to person. For Kiana, the color peach means sweetness but also energy and vitality.
58-59 Pink is the most romantic of romantic colors, always evoking a sweet, dreamlike dimension in any creation.

Yellow: To many, vibrant yellow is reminiscent of the sun, honey, or the scent of lemons. It often symbolizes happiness, optimism, and life itself. "Yellow can brighten a room, and spring is the triumph of all yellows, with its narcissus, ranunculus, and primroses," Kiana says. "Yellow is also one of my preferred colors for my summer floral arrangements, because it makes me happy and leads me to roses, hyacinths, and monkey orchids, which I find particularly funny. In fall, this color makes me think of ginkgo leaves, which remind me of the wonderful fans that I saw in Japan, but also of Icelandic poppies, or American bittersweet vines, whose golden berries ripen into orange later in the season. Yellow is definitely a color to play with, because it carries a touch of joy in both flowers and fruits."

Red: And what about red, the universal hue of love and passion in all its nuances, ranging from the most intense red that tends toward black, to the vibrant, sensual red evoking the color of blood? For Kiana, "Red is always an interesting color to work with. I don't prefer red roses, but I do love the rhododendron and the Indian mallow. In summer, I devote myself to red tulips, sweet peas, anemones, and peach fruits. In fall, I find reds in the turning leaves of trees and in pomegranates. In winter, I mostly look for purple red."

"Many of my compositions are created using a kenzan. I prefer it not only because it produces a natural and draping effect, but also because I think it's more eco-friendly than floral foam. I also use vases that I paint myself and combine them with a rich and varied palette of colors with different types of flowers and natural elements. My favorites are often the stemmed vases, including urns and bowls on short pedestals, in both classic and modern styles. I favor these, as fresh flowers can spring out from all sides in a natural way."

"How would I define my style? Rich, colorful, and complex. I believe all flowers are beautiful; there is no such thing as an ugly flower. You simply have to find the right combination for each. I like working with a wide palette of colors. When I start an arrangement, I must have in front of me a wide variety of shapes and sizes of flowers, so I can choose the best ones to satisfy my inspiration. With today's modern floriculture and ease of shipping, it's possible to get every variety of flower year-round, but I generally try to work with only the varieties available in the country I'm in. For example, I was once in Mexico and couldn't find poppies—so I replaced them with bachelor buttons and local jasmine, which could be found everywhere in the markets and had the most extraordinary perfume."

60–61 Perhaps the most famous of all flowers is the rose, linked to love, in all its nuances.

63 A revelation to the eye, with not a single color missing: from the blue of the gentians, through the pink of the tulips, to the pale yellow of the daffodils.

64 There are many dahlia forms that look like colored balls, filling any corner of the house with joy.

65 A yellow vase, lilac fabric, and then the flowers, bringing life with their pink, fuchsia, peach, yellow, and salmon hues.

"I am known for my bold approach to color and for choosing a wide variety of shades in my flower arrangements, but I also love playing with monochromatic color palettes. I love nuance, and there is so much in nature that we are spoiled by all the choices: from pink to peach, yellow to orange, red to purple . . . There is no limit to creativity. You can use infinite variations within the same color. You can experiment with different lengths and shapes, such as with alternations of light and shadow or with particular backgrounds. And often the most seemingly banal creations become the most intriguing. Never be afraid to dare, to be different; love freedom and color."

"Like vases, backdrops can really create and define a big picture. They are a kind of stage set in which everything takes place, exactly like a show at the theater. In the limited time I find between work and raising a family, I have also tried to paint my own backdrops. I must admit that I enjoy it greatly. The process is for me almost therapeutic, and the result gratifying. I enjoy the silence of the moment! Don't be afraid, don't limit your art to what you know. Never stop creating! And remember that the secret to success is to block out the distraction of the noise around you. Focus on what you set out to achieve, aware that there will be obstacles along the way. Your goal must be to pursue the best version of yourself, now and in the future!"

"Evolution. Allowing yourself room to continually evolve as an artist always yields fresh results, whereas simply recreating old designs or copying others leads only to stagnation. When creating designs, don't be afraid to push your limits and take risks. Be brave and challenge what is traditionally accepted. Aim to be different."

Yet even for weddings, Kiana never follows a predetermined, clearly defined plan, instead taking her inspiration from the different situations she works in, the ceremony location, the couple's love story, or the emotions she senses.

"In weddings, you have to adapt your work to different situations. For example, the celebration of the ceremony might take place in a church, an officiant's office, on a beach or in a garden, or in the most original and unexpected locations. I'm always open and willing to satisfy all the desires of the bride and groom, because I know that when they rely on Tulipina, they want to see art and harmony and to make their wedding a high-quality design moment that people will talk about for a long time. They usually know my brand and what to expect in every respect, and they want something special and unique."

Kiana understands that her designs must work together with the larger vision. "On the wedding day, even the smallest detail plays an important role, even more so for the bride, who must be perfect in every detail, from her wedding gown and veil to shoes, jewels, makeup, and hairstyle. Trying to harmonize my style with all of this—the ceremony and reception venues, the bride and groom's clothing style—is the greatest challenge for me every time, and I face this challenge with all my energy, the experience I've acquired over the years, the love for my job, and my overwhelming passion for the floral universe."

Kiana works with inexhaustible enthusiasm, approaching every element with great dedication. "The bouquet is what the bride holds in her hands, what she constantly sees during the ceremony, and what accompanies her to the altar where her husband-to-be waits for her. It must represent her concept of love, her view of life, and the magic of the moment. The choice of colors is extremely important, but the symbolic meaning is even more so."

"I always prefer to be direct and say clearly that if someone wants to organize a wedding with me, they must be willing to dare. I can't work with clients who won't leave me free to use my rich, sometimes overabundant, style, because I feel I couldn't make their dreams come true. My art is not a simple floral decoration; mine is creation and creativity, free expression. Anyone who turns to me knows they will have something unique and magical, something that has never been seen before."

185 *A bride's bouquet is an essential element, one that must reflect her emotions and dreams. Image courtesy of Corbin Gurkin.*

186-187 *Roses in a bouquet express love better than any other element. Here they are accompanied by small white flowers, symbols of innocence and purity.*

187 *A dress translucent with lace, set off by a near-transparent veil, calls for a bouquet in delicate, muted shades of antique pink. The effect is exquisitely romantic.*

Whenever Kiana speaks with a bride, she tries to understand her values and her concept of matrimonial union. "I mainly rely on this, and I trust my instinct in choosing the best flowers for her. Sometimes they are different from what she imagined, but if she tells me, 'This is the bouquet of my dreams!' (and thankfully, that often happens), my heart is filled with joy! I too have been a bride, and I haven't forgotten anything about that day: the nervousness, the happiness, all the emotions . . ."

188 An opulent bouquet in a theme of creamy white, pink, and fuchsia evokes passion and liveliness, but also sweetness. Image courtesy of Corbin Gurkin.
189 Regal touches of smoky violet balanced by the freshness of peaches and cream form an original and romantic bouquet.

190 *This bouquet's fresh green foliage and pink, apricot, and lavender flowers deliciously complement the yellow tulle dress. Image courtesy of Dikha Dheansa.*
191 *A frame of tiny yellow flowers surrounds a pink heart of ranunculus and carnations. Image courtesy of Jose Villa.*
192–193 *Fine-textured foliage and small berries give this sophisticated bouquet a flavor of antiquity. The real stars are the roses!*

"The bride's bouquet is my priority. It doesn't always have to be complicated—sometimes it can be very simple—but I like doing something unexpected and bringing happiness to the bride. It is essential to talk with her, to understand what she wants. You can start with the color, or with a certain type of flower. I must understand what best suits her character, her nature. I am rarely wrong, mainly thanks to the experience I have built up over the years. And when I see a bride smile, happily holding her bouquet close—well, that just fills my heart with joy."

"Red is love, passion, sensuality. It is perhaps an unusual color at a wedding, but it is equally exciting and pervasive. Ranunculus tend to dance better when part of a bouquet, but then there are poppies, which for me are the expression of maximum playfulness and joy."

194 In the West, red is not exactly traditional for a wedding dress. It takes courage and is sure to surprise. The bouquet that accompanies this one demands equally vibrant, passionate hues. Image courtesy of Corbin Gurkin.

196 For this bride, flowers become an accessory to wear—real natural jewelry! Image courtesy of Elizabeth Messina.

198 A beautiful Japanese bride under a "rain" of orange berries. Kiana is passionate about Japan; it is a constant source of inspiration for her.

"I could interpret a wedding in a hundred different ways and still have hundreds more ideas. The possibilities are simply endless. And the lovers I meet become a part of my life forever, because that moment is just as important to me as an artist, and I know that special day will never be forgotten. That's when I think I have the best job in the world. It is then that I feel I truly believe in love and the power of feelings. Having the opportunity to create beauty for what will perhaps be the most memorable day in a couple's life is an immeasurable honor for me."

"I have loved Japan for as long as I can remember. My uncle introduced me to this country when I was a little girl, telling me about its traditions; it has been a real-life love story ever since. I have vintage kimonos that I adore. My longtime dream was to unite my floral design with Japanese culture and beauty. Being able to organize weddings in this beautiful country, as well as in other fascinating places in Asia, such as Korea and Singapore, is a fairy tale come true. I am also very attached to the culture of China. In fact, since I grew up in San Francisco, which has one of the largest Chinatowns in the world, the Chinese and their traditions have long been a part of my life."

200 *A bright bouquet of tender pinks and unexpected foliage tones features a single white flower of enchanting purity.*
201 *A bride in traditional Japanese dress holds a bouquet in soft, subtle tints, framed by a contrasting arch of rich mauves and pinks.*

*"*When planning a wedding, it's fun looking everywhere for inspiration; it makes you pay attention to the details and teaches you to do this in your personal life too.*"*

202 *In this classic bouquet, formal white roses take center stage. A few touches of antique pink lend a refined air. Image courtesy of Catherine Mead.*
203 *An iconic Venetian gondola is transformed into a cornucopia of magnificent flowers to transport a bride on her big day. Image courtesy of Jose Villa.*

"The first time I laid eyes on Venice, I was twenty, and I was enchanted by the beauty of this ancient city of canals. I was in awe; I never imagined that one day, twenty-six years later, my work, which is my life's passion, would bring me back. My heart is filled with joy and gratitude for the gift of being able to work with flowers."

204 *For Kiana, any flowers arranged in vases must seem to "float," hanging suspended without touching the table. Image courtesy of Jose Villa.*
204-205 *For this exceptional location, flowers not only grace the tables but also hang from above, creating a truly scenographic effect. Image courtesy of Gianluca Adovasio.*

The tables and decorations for the ceremony represent an equally ambitious and demanding challenge for Kiana. "For the tables, I often like to make sure that the attention is focused on large vases with pedestals from which flowers can dominate the room and create a movement of wonderful asymmetries clearly visible from various directions. I like to see flowers trembling as if about to fall from the vase, but without touching the table. I love to play with colors and daring, unexpected plays of light and shadow."

For Kiana, everything is important in the magical atmosphere of the moment: lighting, candles, tablecloths, glasses, silverware, dishes, and music. "Working on a wedding is like creating a wonderful museum installation. It's like an arts festival occurring in various locations that allows me to use my imagination without limits. Is this chance to experiment not the most beautiful opportunity an artist can have?"

Kiana points out that, even if she loves to let her imagination and artistic flair run wild, she wants her work to reflect the desires and ideas of the bride and groom. She recognizes that marriage is a very special moment, about two people who fell in love and decided to commit their lives to each other. This is, above all, the bride and groom's moment. It's her job to make their union unforgettable, and she has just one day to do it. "It is a great responsibility for me, and I really don't want to disappoint them. It is as if I could feel the love of the couple inside me, as a source of inspiration, and I'm willing to give it my all. It sometimes happens that, when they come to me, the bride and groom don't know what they really want; then it's up to me to understand and interpret it. If in the end they tell me that they were surprised and enchanted—well, my satisfaction is great, because their appreciation means that I've been able to evoke the magic of their love. Is there anything more wonderful than this for an artist? After all, for me, art must be love before anything else, and I've based my whole life on this even before becoming a floral designer."

Asked who her ideal customers might be, Kiana responds, "Of course, those who give me freedom to decide, work, and create without restrictions and limitations." She has a clear view of her dream wedding: "Happiness, satisfaction, charm, joy, splendor—these are just some of the emotions and qualities I want to evoke on a day that is meant to be forever."

208 *Saying yes to a life together, the couple is surrounded by a fairy-tale abundance of floral arrangements, offering celebratory fountains of color. Image courtesy of Jose Villa.*

209 *An arrangement of lilies in shades of pink and orange grace each bench, nestled in a froth of white. Image courtesy of Jose Villa.*

"From the very first time I laid eyes on Italy, over twenty-five years ago, my dream has always been to have a reason to call this land my home. Now, even though I don't always live here, I really feel that Italy is my home. Tulipina has opened a branch on Lake Como, a wonderful place where I have organized some memorable weddings. I have also lived in other Italian cities. I love Florence enormously, above all for its magnificent art found around every corner, and I adore Venice, where I have created splendid floral arrangements for important events."

210 *Flowers are arranged in a horseshoe shape, the colors ranging from lush pinks to the blue-violet spires of gladioli at the center. Image courtesy of Matteo Coltro.*

211 *A garden of topiary from a bygone era is crowned with a "stage" of flowers forming exuberant peaks. Sprays of pink echo the form, inviting guests to each row of chairs. Image courtesy of Umberto Armiraglio.*

212-213 *Garlands of peonies, the queen of flowers, await the big event in this enchanted place. Image courtesy of K.T. Merry.*

FANTASY GARDEN

Cultivating a World
of Floral Wonder

THE PRESENT AND THE FUTURE: THE ART OF CREATING AND CULTIVATING A GARDEN

"One of the greatest pleasures in life for me is having a garden, working on it and looking after it throughout the seasons. I have learned many things about how to cultivate beautiful blooms in New York, but the most precious thing I have learned is patience."

Audrey Hepburn, who sought peace and serenity in her garden, once said, "To plant a garden is to believe in tomorrow." Flower gardens awaken our senses and stimulate our emotions. In a garden, surrounded by nature's beauty, you can surrender to feelings of pleasure, hope, and well-being. Your eyes are caught by the harmony of colors and the plays of light and shadow. Your nostrils are filled with the intense fragrances of flowers that, charmingly mingled, envelop you in a sort of blissful enchantment.

As her business grew, Kiana began to dream more and more of having her own floral garden. After many years in the Bay Area, Kiana and Nathan found themselves yearning for change. "We wanted land of our own, a beautiful and affordable place where I could create my own garden of wonders. It would be the one I had imagined since my childhood in Persia, which could reflect my life past, present, and future—because the greatest desire Nathan and I have is that our children will continue to cultivate it after us."

It took more than five years for Kiana and Nathan to find their ideal property. "We decided to move to the Catskills, where the now legendary Woodstock concert took place, which has always been a refuge for artists. For us, those mountains about two hours from New York City had something magical. They form part of the Appalachian range, and they are covered with forests, dotted with lakes, and inhabited by deer, bears, and dozens of bird species that accompany your

217 *Kiana in her garden of wonders, the result of so much dedication and passion. Image courtesy of Greg Finck.*
218 *In this area of the garden, daffodils, hyacinths, and tulips grow in an original orderly planting that leaves them free to express themselves.*
221 *An expanse of daffodils, one of the most beloved flowers of spring.*

" Gardening is one of my favorite ways to decompress between weddings. **"**

days with their singing." The climate where they live makes it possible for them to grow wonderful flowers three seasons a year, which means Kiana has a variety of flowers to experiment and work with.

As she began to make plans for their land, she was inspired by gardens that are not too rigidly maintained. "I love gardens that are free, like my spirit. I love those gardens that are cared for with love, but which are not too strict in their structure, so as to let flowers grow spontaneously. I love gardens where flowers grow according to their own will, and seeds are free to mingle with each other, creating meadows full of colored flowers like those portrayed in many paintings that have inspired my imagination. I love gardens where all flowers can feel at home. Gardens full of abundance and surprise."

For Kiana, a big plot of land is not necessary. "The most beautiful garden of wonders must express your personality. Now more than ever it is essential to plant flowers and trees, because to create a garden is also to take care of nature, thus contributing to fighting the global climate crisis and the gray of pavement, which is unfortunately increasingly dominant in big cities today. How beautiful would it be if instead flowers blossomed from every crack in the walls? How magical would it be if all balconies and windows were full of flower boxes and vases? How wonderful would it be if all flat roofs of modern buildings shone with gardens in bloom?"

"Designing with my garden flowers brings me an indescribable sense of joy! There is just nothing like the movement, color, and texture that you get from homegrown flowers and foliage. My daffodils bring me so much joy, and I continue to be amazed at how many different varieties there are. I wait patiently every year for them to emerge again—and they certainly are worth the wait."

"Here is a little show of some of my garden flowers, budding in the springtime . . ."

AUTHORS AND CONTRIBUTORS

Alessandra Mattanza is an author, a screenwriter, and a fine art photographer. She is a contributor and writer for several publishing houses and magazines, including *Cosmopolitan*, *Elle*, *Vanity Fair*, *Forbes*, *F Magazine*, *Natural Style*, *ICON*, and the *Financial Times*, and she collaborates on interviews and mini documentaries for Universal Television and other television networks. She is the author of a wide range of books, including *My New York: Celebrities Talk about the City*, *My Paris: Celebrities Talk about the Ville Lumière*, *Street Art: Famous Artists Talk about Their Vision*, *C215: Christian Guemy Stencil Art*, *Banksy*, *SOS Planet Earth: Voices for a Better World*, *Street Art's Rising Stars: 24 Artists You Should Know*, and *Women Street Artists: 24 Contemporary Graffiti and Mural Artists from Around the World*.

Kiana Underwood is the founder of the floral design studio Tulipina and one of the most sought-after floral designers in the world. She styles flowers for weddings and events and is a distinguished floral artist and teacher. Underwood employs unique color combinations and floral varieties, including fruits and foliage, that set her apart from her contemporaries and draw admirers and floral designers from all over the world to her sold-out workshops and teaching engagements. Originally from Tehran, Iran, she moved to the United States as a teenager and now splits her time between New York City and Lake Como, Italy.

Nathan Underwood is the operational and business mind of Tulipina, managing its event production, global logistics, business development, technology, and finance. He is also the principal photographer behind many of Tulipina's iconic images.

Jose Villa has been named a top wedding photographer by *Martha Stewart Weddings*, *Harper's Bazaar*, *Style Me Pretty*, *Vogue*, and *American Photo Magazine*. His photos have been published in many magazines around the world.

WS White Star Publishers® is a registered trademark property of White Star s.r.l.
© 2023 White Star s.r.l.
Piazzale Luigi Cadorna, 6 - 20123 Milan, Italy
www.whitestar.it

All images belong to Nathan and Kiana Underwood unless otherwise stated.
105, Albert Williams. All Rights Reserved 2023/Bridgeman Images; 108, Christie's Images/©
Albert Williams. All Rights Reserved 2023/Bridgeman Images;
113, Bridgeman Images; 124, Albert Williams. All Rights Reserved 2023/Bridgeman Images;
126, National Trust Photographic Library/Bridgeman Images;
128, Sepia Times/Universal Images Group/Getty Images; 132, Heritage Images/Hulton
Archive/Getty Images; 138, DeAgostini/Getty Images.

Library of Congress Cataloging-in-Publication Data available.

ISBN 978-1-7972-2684-2

Manufactured in China.

Editorial direction by Valeria Manferto De Fabianis.
Design by Paola Piacco.

10 9 8 7 6 5 4 3 2 1

Chronicle Books LLC
680 Second Street
San Francisco, California 94107
www.chroniclebooks.com